TOMORROW'S WORLD

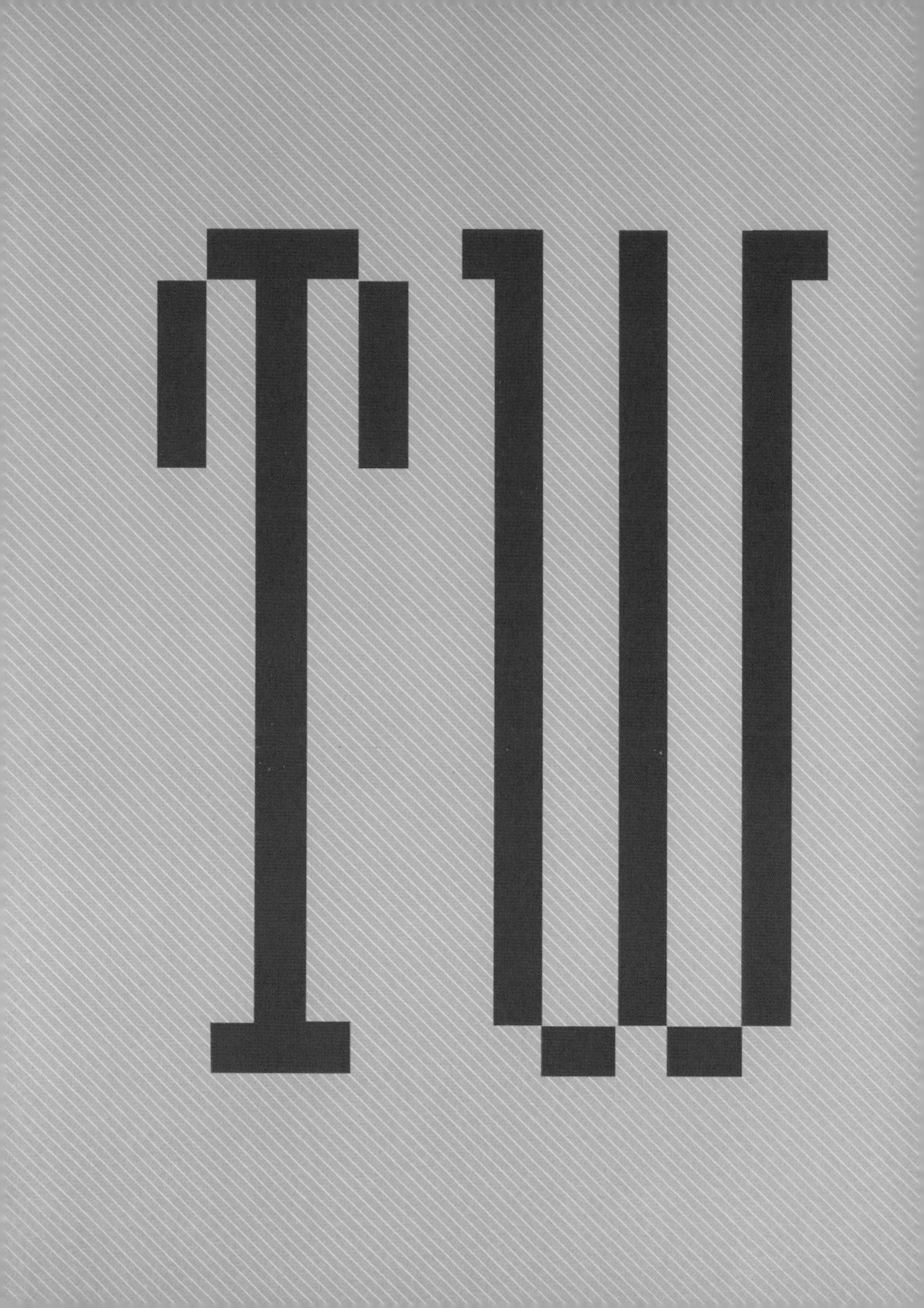
TW

DAVID STUBBS

GENIUS GADGETS AND GIZMOS

Weird & Wonderful Contraptions
from Yesterday's Future

BBC
BOOKS

1 2 3 4 5 6 7 8 9 10

Published in 2008 by BBC Books, an imprint of
Ebury Publishing. A Random House Group Company

The Random House Group Limited Reg. No. 954009

Addresses for companies within the Random House
Group can be found atwww.randomhouse.co.uk

A CIP catalogue record for this book is available from
the British Library.

ISBN 978 1 84 607578 0

Commissioning editor: Lorna Russell
Project editor: Caroline McArthur
Copy-editor: Ian Gittins
Design: Smith & Gilmour, London
Picture researcher: David Stubbs
Production controller: Bridget Fish

Colour origination by: Altaimage, London
Printed and bound in Singapore by Tien Wah Press

CONTENTS

INTRODUCTION

An alternative suggestion for the title of this volume was 'Where's My Jet Pack?' This summarises a grumbling feeling, now that we have landed in the 21st century, that a certain promise made by *Tomorrow's World* has not been made good. Why are we not dressed head to toe in silver, whooshing around the skies to a permanent soundtrack of electronic bleeps and abstract squiggles? Why are our waste-paper bins not talking to us? Why are our toothbrushes not telling us when to stop brushing? Why have buskers not been replaced by robots playing the greatest hits of Walter Carlos and Kraftwerk? Why is there still dirt? Why do we still have to perform our own day-to-day chores, while domestic cybernaut helpers lie idle and half-assembled in research plants closed down due to lack of financing? Why does travel to Mars seem a more remote prospect today than it did 50 years ago?

LEFT The 'Educative Toothbrush' causes a sudden brain surge

RIGHT *TW* presenters contemplate the indispensable gadgets of the 21st century

In fairness, *Tomorrow's World*'s presenters were aware of the invidiousness of their task, and of the weekly hostages they were providing to fortune. They knew that not every single one of their predictions was likely to pan out; not all the inventions they presented would revolutionise our futures. Viewing old episodes from the advantageous position

of hindsight, it's often clear that the presenters were finding it every bit as hard to keep a straight face about some of the inventions they extolled back then as we do now. Conversely, like anyone else who grew up in the 1960s and 1970s, it was hard not to get as caught up as they often did in the white heat of their enthusiasm for the labour-saving gadgets, ultra-modern conveniences and interplanetary space-hops that awaited us all.

Tomorrow's World began in 1965 at a time when Britain, after decades of one form of bleakness or another, was at last beginning to feel good about itself, materially self-confident and forward-looking, as reflected in the music, TV and styles of the day. You could see it in the colours and contours of furniture, in the designs of Mary Quant, in the Union Jack suits of The Who and *The Avengers*. This was a time when to be British was to be ultra-modernistic and high on hope.

Commissioned by one Aubrey Singer, *Tomorrow's World* was conceived on the hoof – the very name of the show was only dreamt up the night before its first ever edition. Despite the swinging times, this was Science on the British Broadcasting Corporation. Raymond Baxter was very much a host of the old school, with his ramrod carriage and bespoke tones, while the narration of Derek Cooper was very much in the 'Look, Listen and Pay Heed'

tradition. However, this was also popular television, and duly leavened with the occasional musical link (including the *Tomorrow's World* song cooed by Lynda Baron in her pre-Nurse Gladys days). There were game stabs at low comedy designed to amuse the common man in items such as the one demonstrating 'ear defenders': noise-cancelling earphones for those working in high-decibel conditions. To demonstrate their efficacy, the young presenter climbed into a large dustbin into which a firework was tossed, only for him to emerge in that sooty and dishevelled but still-alive way that comedy people used to survive explosions back in the 1960s.

By the 1970s, and in tandem with *Top of the Pops*, which followed it on Thursday evenings, *TW* was part of a futuristic continuum, feeding spangly fantasies of the 21st century technocracy to come, whether envisaged by a Baxter or a Bolan. This was its heyday, when it attracted some ten million viewers, even if a proportion of them were bored pop-pickers waiting for Judith Hann to stop banging on about advances in washing-machine technology so that they could see Slade. By the 1980s however, as we lived in an increasingly synthesized soundtrack world and computers and silicon chips were becoming increasingly everyday items, the future didn't seem quite so far off. If there was a turning point for the show, it may have been the 'Hissing Sid' item. Initially intended, you suspect, as a serious item

LEFT Headphones test. Which is louder, Lulu's 'Boom Bang-a-Bang' or an actual bang?

RIGHT Inflatable mashed potato will mean more than enough to go round

about a snooker-playing robot, presenter Kieran Prendiville initially seemed put out when Sid the robot effectively corpsed in the limelight. However, he quickly salvaged the item, turning it into a comedy celebration of technology's fallibility, or even its outright uselessness. The show was, thereafter, gently vinegared with a sense of irony.

The Hissing Sid debacle also highlighted something else quite remarkable about *Tomorrow's World*: that, for most of its history, the show went out live. This would have been of little matter to a stalwart like Raymond Baxter – there had been no rehearsal for the Second World War, why should there be one for a TV programme about the hover-cars of the future? However, it tested the nerves of some young producers, such as Allan Lee. 'The potential for disaster in a live programme of this nature is always just around the corner,' he wrote in 2001. 'If a gizmo doesn't work, or it takes too long to warm up, or it goes wrong and blows up (and that's happened more than once), then the presenters have to be able to keep the show on the rails and still end it on time. The cardinal sin was to overrun your slot, and make the whole of the rest of the network run late.'

By the 1990s, the show's original theme, a sleek, reassuring Johnny Dankworth instrumental that could easily have been the soundtrack to a DIY programme or quiz show, had long since been displaced by a more turbo-charged techno theme. This was appropriate. The world was no longer light or jazzy but proceeded at the remorseless pace of a new, digital rhythm. However, the show was hovering somewhere between venerated institution and anachronism. It was clear that the whole trajectory of the future differed from that imagined not just by *TW* but by society as a whole. The revolution was not in 'stuff' so much as the means by which stuff was conveyed and disseminated: communications technology in general, and the Internet in particular.

LEFT Bulletproof vest, with bonus chin protection

Cars were clearly destined to remain earthbound and space travel had, like so many other would-be giant leaps for mankind, been hamstrung as the spirit of adventure was replaced by the spirit of accountancy. There was a last fit of enthusiasm at the dawn of the millennium in which, during a series of specials headed by Peter Snow, the programme posited, with a mixture of heady excitement and underlying irony, the notion that robot domestic help, flying cars and improbable developments in the Internet such as special 'E-Suits', would all be with us soon. However, it was hard to square this with the show's own admonitions about global warming, which haunted most people's perceptions of the coming decades. The show was finally cancelled in 2003, with its spirit only revived by the cruel parodists of the Look Around You series.

It should not be forgotten that *TW* had a decently high hit rate in judging What Life Will Be Like in the 1990s and Beyond. It wasn't just global warming and the perils of the 'aerosol age', which it flagged up as early as 1984. Among its correct predictions were, famously, the compact disc, but also the breathalyser, clockwork radio, digital watch, bulletproof vest, mobile phone, Walkman, bagless vacuum cleaner, the metal detector innovations of John Adams, implants for epileptics and, way back in 1975, the idea that popular music would be transformed by four grave young German men in suits with a distaste for guitars. It would be fair to give equal prominence to these frequent moments of foresight, as well as to acknowledge that the presenters and makers of the show were, in the main, rather frighteningly clever people who, far from deserving light mockery, did a tremendous and perhaps under-appreciated job in popularising modern science as well as they did for so long. It's to their efforts that this volume, which has no intention whatsoever of being fair, is humbly dedicated.

RAYMOND BAXTER

With his plummy gravitas coupled with a benevolent twinkle of the eye, Raymond Baxter WAS *Tomorrow's World* so far as those of a certain generation are concerned. He was the original presenter and tone-setter. As a former Spitfire pilot and a man who had performed radio commentary on the funeral of King George VI and the coronation of Queen Elizabeth II, he was a fellow of intrepid adventure and a safe pair of Establishment hands. Underlying his feature items, assisted by his trusty Parker pen pointer, was the reassurance that whatever shape the future took, it would be in the best and most solid of British traditions: occasionally eccentric but fundamentally sensible, with cause for measured excitement but not for alarm. Sadly, in 1977 Baxter fell out with young *TW* editor Michael Blakstad, who described him as a 'dinosaur'. However, he was brought back into the fold in the 1990s to present special feature items such as 'Raymond's Rock 'n' Roll Years', in which he gamely name-checked pop luminaries such as Yazz and Annie Lennox as he looked back on *TW*'s heyday. He died in 2006.

JAMES BURKE

'Get James Burke on the case', the Human League once urged us, and thankfully, ever since first appearing on *Tomorrow's World* in the 1960s, he's never been off it. Born in Northern Ireland, James Burke has an impressive CV as a science historian, author and documentary producer. He brought a light, populist touch to his *TW* enthusiasm for technological innovation and was always happy to don a silly hat or take part in comedy stunts if it helped us further understand the role things like carbon fibre would play in our future day-to-day lives. When introduced to the show, he added a certain youthful vigour and a pair of enormous black-rimmed spectacles that contained much of the televisual essence of Burke. Having been the main presenter on the BBC's coverage of the moon landings in 1969, Burke became practically synonymous with popular TV science. However, in more recent years, despite having apparently evaporated from our screens, he has enjoyed transatlantic success with his long-running series *Connections*, first broadcast in 1979, and as an eminent science writer.

TOMORROW'S
LEISURE AND STYLE

WHAT WILL
WE DO WHEN
IT'S ALL DONE
FOR US ?

One of the tenets to which *TW* held fast even until the year 2000 was that the future would bring a great deal more free time to the average person, what with the man-hours saved by microchips, right down to the man-seconds saved by curtains that opened and shut themselves. The *Tomorrow's World Annual* of 1970 mused confidently on the 'super-abundance of leisure time' we could all expect to enjoy in the coming decades, while in the late 1970s, trade union leader Sid Weighell predicted on *TW* that his members would soon be working 24-hour weeks. Today's stressed British workforce might emit a hollow laugh at these sanguine projections, but it might console them, as they hang from a strap on a 21st-century cattle truck, enduring after-hours work-related earache on their mobile phones, that somewhere in a parallel universe, the Future That Never Was offers leisure options in droves.

Rather more on the mark was *TW*'s prediction of the future state of the leisured masses. Here is what they said in 1970. Any of this strike a chord? 'You will travel a great deal more and in general spend a great deal more money (and you will eventually forget what cash is and regard debt as a very necessary means of keeping the national economy healthily productive). You will be physically healthier, but probably a good deal more on the edge as the tempo of living quickens. In fact, a day in your tomorrow will make parts of your life very much easier and other parts that you have never considered important very much more difficult.'

RIGHT Go on in, you know it makes sense

THE FUN PALACE

Tomorrow's World's 1970 annual, casting around for things we might do as our cyber-skivvies rushed around picking up our discarded socks, cited the idea devised by one Keith Albarn of a 'Fun Palace'. This would consist of a 'collection of brilliantly coloured plastic domes held together by plastic bolts; the interior is a series of womb-like chambers linked by tubular corridors'. The idea was to offer visitors a 'total experience', bombarding them with changing sounds, stroboscopic light patterns, different wall textures and moving floors. There was an early stab at interactivity: special panels would be set up, enabling you to create your own 'sound and light' show. 'It should be an intriguing place to spend a quiet Sunday afternoon', remarked the annual, justifiably reflecting the mood of elation. Sadly, although some of Albarn's ideas have filtered through, here we are in the future and we are sadly short of the Fun Palaces he envisaged. Indeed, the fate of the Millennium Dome showed that we Brits would rather spend our Sundays in slow-moving traffic looking for parking spaces outside PC World than have any truck with Fun Palaces.

THE COMPUTER ROWING MACHINE

In 1984, fitness fanatics were still reeling from the news that Jim Fixx, pioneer of the jogging craze, had dropped dead aged just 52, and were sniffing around for safer and more hi-tech ways to minimise their circumferences. *TW* responded with a somewhat rudimentary-looking rowing machine that, by today's standards, essentially consisted of a couple of metal sticks and a giant elastic band. The problem was that exercising on the thing was tedious. 'However,' presenter Peter Macann smirked in one of *TW*'s occasional regrettable forays into scatological punning, 'this machine has a few tricks up its rollocks.' The trick in this case was that it linked up to a computer screen whose snaky strip of neon blue indicated a river down which the rower could 'virtually' progress as they heave-hoed – a delightful aid to offset boredom. Visual electronic luxury, in fact, although tell that to today's youngsters with their PlayStations and they'd think you were having a laugh, like.

LEFT Jolly virtual boating weather

RIGHT Judith Hann fails to afford the Squash Ball Warmer the gravitas it deserves

THE SQUASH-BALL-WARMING MACHINE

There is little to say about the squash-ball-warming machine (designed to end once and for all the hours spent, and back-breaking drudgery endured, warming up your own damn balls) except that it is perhaps the single most pathetic invention ever to have featured on *Tomorrow's World*. Even Judith Hann, normally a model of grave, professional composure, took several takes before she could introduce the item without collapsing in giggles. Thanks to the existence of a basic level of human shame about doing some things yourself (the electronic backside-wiper never took off for the same reason), this one never caught on.

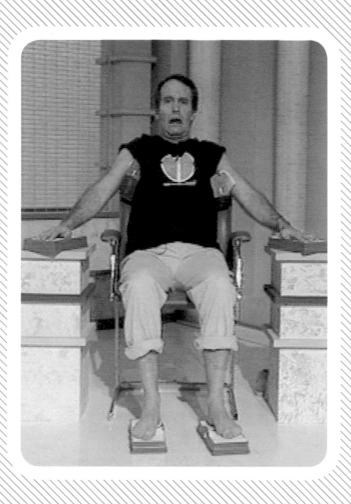

THE JOGGER AIR-WARMER

For those who insisted on persisting with what Jim Fixx had shown to be the almost certainly fatal pursuit of jogging, Kieran Prendiville mooted this invention, a sort of hyperventilating contraption that would provoke even the dogs to laugh at you in the park. To his credit, Prenders didn't disguise his bewilderment at the thing. 'It's supposed to warm up the air that joggers breathe while they're running,' he offered, though the benefit of this remained obscure. Shares in the product did not, ultimately, hold up well.

THE ELECTRONIC ANTI-PERSPIRANT

Clearly, there would be so little to do in the future that it's hard to see how anyone would build up a sweat. However, just in case they did, help was on hand from California. By clasping absorbent, pore-suppressing blue blocks to your armpits, hands and feet for eight half-hour sessions, you could go for six weeks without so much as a trickle of perspiration. In case you're sweating with tension right now, wondering whether it caught on or not, the answer is, 'Hell, no!'

THE HOLIDAY COMPUTER

Well, this one *TW* got half right. In their 1970 annual they suggested that here, in the future, we would determine our vacations by means of a 'specially programmed computer' that would help us make our choices. Do you prefer driving, flying or sailing? What kind of scenery would Sir or Madam like? To help, the computer would flag up images of various choices – sunset on the waves, snow-capped mountains turning pink, a village belfry sinking into darkness. Strangely, the vision of hordes of drunken Essex youths 'having it large' in Ibiza was not one it envisaged.

LEFT Another *TW* first – viewers vote for
a presenter to be sent to the electric chair

TOMORROW'S GIRL

In 1965, one question above all vexed those of a modern-minded bent as they peered curiously at the unwritten pages of the 1970s, 1980s and 1990s – just how would the young ladies of tomorrow turn themselves out in order to please their menfolk? Raymond Baxter felt he had the answer, and presented to viewers a demure young thing, assuring us that she was the embodiment of 'Tomorrow's Girl'. At first glance, it was if the word 'tomorrow' was to be taken literally as, aside from an asymmetrical hairstyle, she was 1965 incarnate in plastic chic. However, all was not as it seemed. Take her shirt, for instance – it was made of paper: 'Ideal for jotting down numbers'. Well, you know what you girls are like, constantly scribbling on your own clothes. Furthermore, those earrings weren't earrings but tiny transistor radios, one of them tuned, this being a female, to the Light Programme. At least Mr Baxter fell short of predicting that by 2000, all women would be replaced by robots.

LEFT Tomorrow's Girl looks well pleased with her haircut

RIGHT Tomorrow's Girl listens to *Housewives' Choice* on her transistor earrings

ABOVE Raymond gets frisky

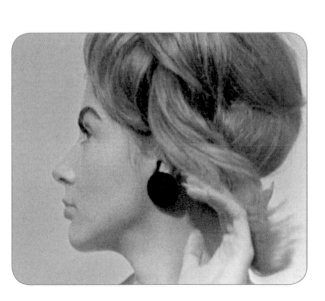

THE SOLAR ALUMINIUM TRAP

Invented by one Brenda Carter, this was considered rather a success in 1975, the year it was first exhibited on *Tomorrow's World*. By trapping and refracting the sun's rays, the aluminium trap afforded even those unlucky enough to live at a British seaside resort the holiday of their dreams, even in unseasonable August. 'You could well be in St Tropez,' enthused the voiceover as a sunglasses-sporting Ms Carter relaxed in a trap of her own devising. 'No need to send your wife on a Mediterranean holiday!' Instead, just order her to spend a fortnight sitting inside a giant tin can in her own back garden, and see how long it takes before she tries to take out your eye with a flying wedding ring.

LEFT The solar hut and spare tyre. Why bother going on a real holiday?

RIGHT It's Philippa's galaxy and we're just living in it

THE 3-D TELEVISION

In 2000, Philippa Forrester donned a piece of the headgear imagined by many to be mandatory in the 21st century and predicted the onset of a new form of television, one then being developed in Japan – the three-dimensional variety, in which on-screen objects were given an 'insect eye' effect by thousands of lenses filming from thousands of different angles. She also promised that by 2007, TVs would contain computers that would enable us to schedule our 'favourite programmes'. True enough, we can now do this. The only problem is finding programmes that could credibly be preceded by the word 'favourite'. As for 3-D TV, the domination of celebrity culture on our screens means that most of the time we have two superfluous dimensions left over.

THE FLYING DUSTBIN AND OTHER JUNK DREAMS

From electric rollerskates to inflatable giant hamster wheels, developments in transportation always provided *Tomorrow's World* with some of its most impressive, but also least thought-through inventions. From its outset, *TW* tapped into a general sense, encouraged by 1960s developments in space travel and the jet pack featured in the Bond movie *Thunderball*, that in the future we would spend a great deal of our time roughly 90 feet in the air. No one really considered whether this was practical or affordable, or even particularly desirable. It just seemed cool, in a Dan Dare/Jetsons sort of way. Nor has the failure of contraption after contraption to make any realistic headway put a lid on the grumbling one frequently hears from we poor souls who find ourselves landed up in the 21st century: 'Why can't my car fly?'

LEFT Reinventing the wheel

RIGHT **William Woollard beholds the Skyship with awe**

THE FLYING SAUCER

Yes, an actual flying saucer. In 1975, William Woollard wore his blackest and widest kipper tie to introduce this item, to emphasise just what a momentous day this was in aeronautical history. The British, showing that anything little green men could do they could do better, had manufactured the first flying saucer. Designed by John West (not to be confused with the tuna man), the Skyship was a 30 foot diameter scale model and was first demonstrated at an aircraft hangar in Cardington. West planned to produce a 200-foot diameter machine with a six-to-ten-ton payload. It would be able to travel as far as a thousand miles at almost a hundred miles per hour. Vectored thrust from its fan jets would be used for docking. Woollard was especially impressed by the saucer's low operating costs, compared to a conventional jet aircraft. And so, even as the scale model descended impotently to ground level behind him in the hangar like a three-day-old party balloon, appearing at one point to be in danger of bursting on one of Woollard's lapels, it was clear that this was the future: We Were The Aliens Now! But then, along came punk rock and the Thatcher years, and the Skyship, like so many 1970s things, was forgotten.

THE INFLATABLE RIVER-CROSSER

This handy device was first exhibited at the Brighton Festival in 1970. It featured 12 inflatable tetrahedrons, which were essentially 15-feet-tall air envelopes in which local men were invited to walk across the sea between Brighton's West and Palace Piers. Essentially intended to be an art exhibit that would 'change people's conceptions about water', *TW* took a far more practical line on the whole thing. Their conception about water didn't need changing: they knew it was wet, and – unless you were the Messiah – impossible to walk on. However, what these inflatables *did* represent was a boon to the harassed metropolitan commuter. And so James Burke was duly kitted out with bowler hat, briefcase and copy of the *Financial Times*, and sealed in the air envelope before being pushed out for a bumpy ride across the Thames. As he cavorted and collapsed inside the tetrahedron, which for all the control he had over it could have been transporting him many miles downriver in the direction of Southend, you suspect that even sanguine futurist Mr Burke might have realised that this wasn't going to be the 21st-century replacement for the number 9 bus.

THE HELICAR

This was presented as the dream of every disgruntled motorist stuck in traffic. Simply press a button and rotor-blades instantaneously unpack on the roof, transforming your motor vehicle into . . . the helicar. This soaraway sensation was, intoned the *TW* voiceover, so simple to operate that even your secretary would be capable of managing the relevant levers! There have been a number of attempts to produce flying motor vehicles, all of them seized upon with alacrity by *TW* over the years. There was the aerocar, for example, produced as early as 1949. Essentially it was a road automobile to which wings could be attached, converting it into an ersatz light aircraft. However, only six were ever produced. The absence of flying cars is one respect in which a great many people feel that they have been short-changed by the 21st century. However, in the rush of blood to the head that comes with contemplating airborne driving, the basic impracticalities of air traffic control that would ensue tend, initially at least, to be disregarded. We don't care! We want our flying cars!

RIGHT How we will all be getting about by the year 1977

LEFT The battle is on to reach the other side of the Thames before the bubble reaches Southend

THE FLYING BICYCLE

As early as 1909, the *New York Times* reported the speculations of a Mr Bois, who asserted with some certainty that the motor car would be rendered obsolete a hundred years hence. 'Mr. Bois believes that a kind of flying bicycle will have been invented which will enable everybody to traverse the air at will, far from the Earth,' it explained.

'Pneumatic railways and flying cars and many other means of quick transit will be so developed that the question of time will enter but little into one's choice of a home.' The Wright Brothers' first attempts at aviation were essentially flying bicycles, but by the late 1960s *Tomorrow's World* was still able to muster a sense of wonder at a draped craft that could be 'pedalled into the air by the muscle power of a single cyclist'. One can only assume that a combination of a generous wind on the day and the billowing drapes played their part in the enterprise for, while this particular vehicle took off, with the exception of E.T., the flying bicycle never did.

THE JET PACK

It was the 1965 James Bond film *Thunderball* that first introduced the jet pack to the world. Cinema fans and techno-enthusiasts rubbed their hands with glee and looked forward to a distant 1970s and 1980s when we would be roaring around all over the shop, scattering the sparrows as we made our merry way hither and yon. Sadly, what the film-makers artfully concealed was that the jet pack was only able to function for a maximum of 21 seconds – possibly enough time to make a quick trip to the corner shop for a packet of 20 Benson & Hedges, but no more than that. It was hardly worth donning the fireproof body suit for. Yet *TW* monitored the progress of the jet pack since this was the sort of stuff, rather than boring

LEFT You'll believe a man can't fly

RIGHT AND BELOW Future Man heads for pub, overshoots. The rocket belt. We want ours!

old advances in the field of zinc mining, that its viewers really craved. A jet packer featured in the opening ceremony of the 1984 Olympic Games, but the technology has never really developed. As recently as July 2007 an American company was manufacturing jet packs, but they would set you back $155,000 and keep you airborne for just 33 seconds.

THE FLYING DUSTBIN

The jet pack may have plummeted quickly down to earth but hopes of energy-wasting, exercise-avoiding, socially irresponsible one-man airborne travel were boosted in 1983, when *TW* was able to report on the development of what its makers rather humourlessly insisted on naming the Wasp II, but what everyone else knew as the Flying Dustbin. With its turbofan engine, a modified version of that used in a cruise missile, it was able to reach speeds of 60 mph and stay airborne for half an hour. Because you stood in it, rather than having it strapped to your back like the dull old jet pack, it was able to carry more fuel in its side panels. The Flying Dustbin

LEFT Bye-bye wheelies – the Flying Dustbin

RIGHT New train technology actually works shock

certainly looked like tremendous fun, and could have, despite the first six or seven attempts in which the passenger fell backwards out of the bin on take-off, breaking several bones, played its part in adding to the ease and comfort of modern life. Sadly, as *TW*'s Howard Stableford solemnly noted in 1995, the Flying Dustbin was 'trashed'. Today, an example of this relic of futures past is on display in Japan's Strange Mechanism Museum.

THE ADVANCED PASSENGER TRAIN

In the swinging 1960s and supersonic 1970s, talk of the Advanced Passenger Train was on everybody's lips. What excited commuters most was its tilting mechanism, which enabled the train to maintain high speeds even when taking corners. The APT eventually hit the tracks in the early 1980s. Sadly however, it encountered problems almost immediately. It wasn't the tilting mechanism that was the problem but the other swanky little state-of-the-art features its makers could not resist installing. These included its hydrokinetic brakes, which unfortunately, Britain being Britain, had an alarming tendency to freeze. While a brakeless train is undeniably fun to watch, it is rather less fun to be inside. Then again, the malfunctions of the APT were such that, mostly, it simply sat in the station awaiting a replacement engine from Crewe. By 1988 the APT had been scrapped, taking with it the dreams of a previous generation. However, in later years other European countries, even a Mussolini-less Italy, were able to develop their own effective APTs, and Richard Branson has succeeded in reviving the technology on his Virgin rail network. Now all he needs is a tilting mechanism on the coaches that carry you for half of your journey during Christmas and Easter holidays and he's laughing.

THE ELECTRIC CAR

As a small boy, watching *Tomorrow's World*, the frequently recurring subject of the electric car intrigued me. I felt I detected one rather obvious drawback – the length of the extension lead required to keep it connected to the plug socket. In truth, the real difficulties facing the electric car have been not much less insurmountable. The best that Michael Rodd could offer in the 1980s was 55 miles at 30 mph before recharging: not the sort of figures to have the petroleum companies quaking in their boots, or Jeremy Clarkson jumping up and down with girlish excitement. It doesn't help that, for some reason, the manufacturers of the electric car insist on putting them out in such ridiculous designs, as if hell-bent on failure and public mockery. *TW* has always kept faith with electric cars, however, even in the darkest depths of their silliness, and is vindicated at last: in Paris there is a scheme afoot for a fleet of 'short-hop' electric motor vehicles, as well as recharging stations, so that the capital's citizens can merrily trundle around the Place de la Concorde, waving their fists at one another.

LEFT The electric car – a phallic thimble

RIGHT Will there be room for you in there, Michael?

THE FLYING WING

The flying wing has been in development since the 1940s, but in the 1990s *TW* reported on a breakthrough that saw a new prototype launched, capable of an air speed of 65 mph. The advantages of the flying wing are its aerodynamic efficiency, lacking as it does a fuselage or vertical stabiliser. However, the disadvantage, as *TW*'s demonstration rather worryingly illustrated, was that the flying wing doesn't appear to be terribly stable. Plus, well, it's just a wing. Where are the in-flight entertainment, the luggage, the trolleys, the duty-free items, the vomit bags, oh, and the people supposed to go? Or, indeed, the other wing?

THE REUSABLE ROCKET

Houston, we have a turkey. Developed in the mid-1990s, the DC-X reusable rocket was pioneered in the true 'waste not, want not' spirit of space travel. Its first test launch was in 1993. The good news was that it came back down to earth intact. The bad news was that it only managed to ascend 100 feet. The second time it was launched, it suffered an explosion in its side panelling. By 1995, *TW* was able to report that on its most recent launch it just about managed to go higher than you could throw a stone into the air, and hopes were raised that this test vehicle could prove a breakthrough in orbital travel, eventually leading to cheap and affordable holidays on Mars. Sadly, by 1996 funding of the reusable rocket was terminated, and the DC-X went out of production.

LEFT The flying wing – it never really took off

RIGHT The DC-X rocket just prior to descent – impressive

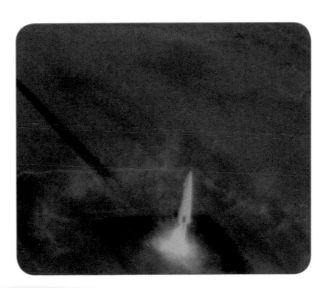

THE VERTICAL TAKE-OFF PASSENGER PLANE

Almost 30 years ago, *Tomorrow's World* assured its audience that by now, passenger planes would take off in a manner akin to the Harrier Jump Jet, thereby precluding the need for long runways. The modern passenger, staring out of his window at those little things on the ground that look like ants and realising that, what with the ruddy plane still trundling round in a traffic jam 40 minutes after scheduled take-off time, they *are* ants, is arguably entitled to an ironic laugh here. Although a disc-shaped vertical take-off aircraft is at the development stage in the US, this is intended to perform helicopter-style rescue missions. The vertical take-off passenger plane remains the aeronautical equivalent of the jet pack.

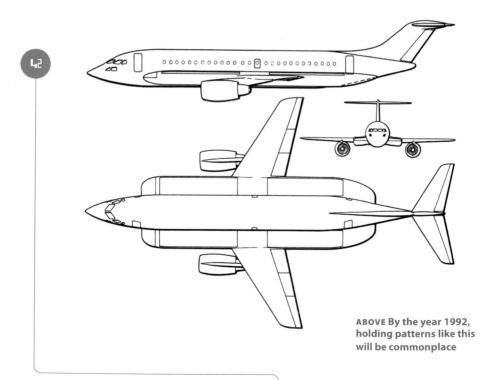

ABOVE By the year 1992, holding patterns like this will be commonplace

THE PERSONAL HELICOPTER

Developed in Japan, the GEN H-4 was – indeed, is – a safer, if sillier, option than the jet pack, and enables the rider to stay airborne for 30 minutes, travelling at speeds of 60 mph. It looks like a tripod with a winch applied up and between the legs, which might prove uncomfortable in the event of a sudden, upward gust of wind. Rotor-blades 13 feet long and two small cylinder engines help set you afloat, with the inventors claiming that the GEN H-4 is as easy to operate as a bicycle. It costs $32,000, which some consider a bit steep, and it has to be said that although they appear still to be in production, the skies are not exactly black with the things. Philippa Forrester reported for *TW* on the personal helicopter, even venturing out to the plant in Japan where it was manufactured. However, her enthusiasm fell short of actually having a go on one of them. I bet Judith Hann would have done.

THE MOVING PAVEMENT

Debuted at the Great Exhibition in Paris in 1889 as *'le trottoir roulant'*, the moving pavement was a great success, and the inexplicable failure to introduce it everywhere is a source of much resentment among modern citizens. *Seinfeld*'s George Costanza summed up the mood of his generation. 'We could be zipping about all over the place!' he seethed, bewailing their absence. This is all the more poignant as, in the early 1970s, *Tomorrow's World* declaimed 'there is no doubt' that moving walkways would exist for the convenience of the pedestrians of the future 'in mass use in every urban area'. As things stand, however, they are generally only used for the acceleration of passengers who've misread the departure gate signs at airports. Yet, on reflection, George Costanza does have a point. Given that nowadays we'd have a good chance of overtaking most city traffic which, in London in particular, moves slower than in the horse-drawn era, moving pavements would be a cracking idea. Time, perhaps, to pound our metaphorical knives and forks on the table and shout out to the city planners: 'Why are we waiting?'

THE THRUST CAR

In the mid-90s, Richard Noble OBE was the King of Thrust. He developed The Thrust2, which broke the land speed record in Black Rock Desert, Nevada, in 1997. A thrusting achievement indeed, which thrust Britain to the forefront of supersonic land travel. The key to his success was thrust – and, if at thrust you don't succeed, then thrust, thrust and thrust again. In 1995, *TW* followed the thrust of his progress towards eventual success, showing a demonstration of his thrust technology, which had male viewers thrusting the air in admiration. A quite magnificent and useful development in vehicular travel around London, especially if, due to some future thrust-related reproductive crisis, the city's population should fall below 100.

LEFT Baxter gets ready to thrust

RIGHT The SSC 2 – it's British and it's a whopper

ABOVE The SSC Test – change of trousers for Mr Clarkson

JUDITH HANN

The late 1970s and 1980s were times of great social and technological upheaval. Thankfully, there was one reassuring constant throughout this period, and that was Judith Hann's hairdo: a perm in the truest sense of the word. The daughter of former Derby County footballer Ralph Hann, she was *Tomorrow's World*'s first female presenter and exuded a kindly, if slightly schoolmarmish, authority on a range of subjects. If she ever ran the risk of appearing a tad starchy, this was dispelled by items such as the one in which she operated a mechanical contraption designed to repel a scrum of rugby players, whom she duly collapsed with the aid of a lever; the famous rodeo simulator of 1978, which contained just the naughtiest hint of sexual mischievousness; and her demonstration of a swingable champagne tray ('That should surprise the waiters on British Rail!').

Hann eventually became *TW*'s longest-serving presenter. Since leaving the series she has made occasional TV and radio appearances, but has now settled in the Cotswolds, where she cultivates a lifelong and decidedly unfuturistic passion for herbs.

TOMORROW'S WORLD PRESENTERS

48

WILLIAM WOOLLARD

It would be no surprise to learn that Woollard's real name
was actually Archie Blenkinsopp, for so perfectly does the
name William Woollard capture the dashing presenter's
rugged combination of suave machismo and grey-pullover
reliability that it could have been invented for him. He was
equally at home nestled in the leather seat of yet another
prototype flying car, fondly caressing the gear stick, or,
prototype New Man that he was, donning his chef's hat and
presenting an item on The Kitchen Of Tomorrow. Grammar
school- and Oxford-educated, Woollard trained as a fighter
pilot, then worked for an oil company in Beirut, where he
acquired both Arabic and a deep tan. As well as presenting
TW, he fronted both *The Risk Business* and a series entitled
The Secret War, which told the story of the British code-
breakers who deciphered the messages sent by the German
military via Enigma. He also presented *Top Gear* in its rather
less flippant, pre-Jeremy Clarkson days. Today, we have
a culture of laddishness; once, there was such a thing as
manliness, and William Woollard was its epitome.

MICHAEL RODD

Every comprehensive school had a teacher like Michael Rodd:
one whose youthful affability gave him an air of having
recently been a head prefect, a friendly sort but with a touch
of steel beneath the floppy fringe. He was not the sort of
schoolmaster you could hound into a nervous breakdown
and early retirement. Having earned his spurs on *Screen
Test*, the cinema-quiz series that pitted the nation's youthful
cineaste swots against one another, he joined the *Tomorrow's
World* team as another counter to the perceived fustiness
exuded by long-standing presenter Raymond Baxter.

Few other presenters, then or now, would have been
willing to eat a worm omelette on the air. Clearly this was
a man who, if it came to it, would not only stand up well
to torture, but even exhibit a polite interest in the work of
his tormentors ('And how long have you been in this line of
work?'). In 1980, Rodd founded his own company, Blackrod,
which does video and interactive work for business and
industry.

TOMORROW'S
MUSIC YESTERDAY

THE FUTURE
SOUNDS OF
SCIENCE

Music has always been at the heart of the *Tomorrow's World* enterprise. While its own theme tune might not, in its earliest days, have quite struck the futuristic chord you would have hoped for, the programme did keep pace with developments in synthesized sound, even in the days when such instruments filled up two rooms. In 1971, for example, *TW* showcased the 'Musys', declaring it 'One of the latest devices for producing electronic music'. It consisted of five enormous computers, each the size of Tony Soprano's fridge, a keyboard, an electric typewriter, a magnetic tape drive and 'fast paper-tape reader/punch', and composed pieces such as 'Probabilistic Selection No 3', which only the machine itself was capable of playing. However, *TW* was also capable of acknowledging the less daunting, more human side of the music of the coming decades. It was especially fond of characters who had taken traditional instruments and given them some sort of electronic modification, even if these could all too often be filed under 'G' for 'Gimmick'. It did not help the instruments of the future that they were normally introduced to the world by Kieran Prendiville, who tended to extract from them little beyond opportunities for light-heartedness. However, *TW* did feature a number of groups whose future was ahead of them, even if it was somewhat limited (one was Landscape, who had a couple of hits when they went electronic in 1980, including 'Einstein a Go-Go'), as well as the rather more prominent likes of Pink Floyd and, notably, Kraftwerk. Tomorrow's music yesterday . . .

RIGHT **The rarely employed** *Tomorrow's World* **Dancers**

THE TOMORROW'S WORLD DANCERS

In 1986, *Tomorrow's World* showcased a bold attempt to create a synergy between light, colour, movement and sound, the like of which had confounded and eluded great composers and artists such as Scriabin and Kandinsky. Step forward the enthusiastic, leotard-clad *Tomorrow's World* dancers, who, introduced by a considerably less mobile Howard Stableford, engaged in a series of moves which triggered off a musical score made of upsampled, synthesized sounds which were activated as the dancers passed through the appropriate beams. Sadly, this bold attempt at fusion had more of the fission about it: the resulting production, a quarter of a century on, bears the distinct whiff of waste product.

LEFT The Kaleidophone and its inventor – surprisingly unpopular with the ladies

THE KALEIDOPHONE

Such was the name conferred upon this instrument by Raymond Baxter in his voiceover, featured in 1976 and introduced by Judith Hann. It was a modification of the original kaleidophone, invented in the 19th century by Charles Wheatstone. Its 20th-century creator, Matt, a would-be rock star, wanted to play electronic music but circumvent the keyboard in favour of a subtler medium. Hence, he devised what Hann described reverentially as 'a mixed marriage between a violin and a plastic drainpipe'. As the beardy Matt played us out, the very epitome of pre-punk virtuoso complacency, twaddling away on a kaleidophone protruding unapologetically from behind his belt like an electronic codpiece, it felt like prog rock's final extravagance. One can imagine, somewhere in north London, Johnny Rotten turning to his mates Steve Jones and Paul Cook: 'Sod this, lads. Let's form a band!'

RIGHT The Moog synth – complex technology required to make farting noises

THE MOOG SYNTHESIZER

Robert Moog's invention first appeared on *Tomorrow's World* in 1969, played by Michael Vickers. The Moog's place in musical history is assured: Stevie Wonder was among the first pop artists to make wide use of it, and since then it has become part of the essential fabric of popular (and unpopular) music. However, somehow or other, even when *Tomorrow's World* got it right, as they indubitably did here, they still managed to get the wrong end of the stick. Trying to make sense of the multi-purpose instrument, the *TW* voiceover surmised, in *Pathé News* bulletin tones, that 'The days of the one-man band are back.'

LEFT AND BELOW
**Synthesizers? In
rock? No freakin'
way!** *TW* **gets it right**

**RIGHT Kraftwerk's
Ralf Hutter wigs out**

THE AUTOBAHN

In 1975, there was a treat for those pop-pickers who were only sitting through *TW* while they waited for the likes of the Bay City Rollers, and Jasper Carrott doing his 'Funky Moped' on *Top of the Pops*. The programme featured a curious quartet from Düsseldorf who went by the name of Kraftwerk. With their names lit up in neon script

onstage, their bland, jobsworth suits and short, slicked-back hair, they were so straight they were alien. Using electronic keyboards, a confusing array of knobs and consoles and tapping out synthetic rhythms on battered-looking metal objects, they were, apparently, from the future. The song, a voiceover gravely informed us, was called 'Autobahn', the German for 'motorway': 'Inspired by the rhythm of trucks and cars heard while driving through Germany.' Their next plan, apparently, was to dispense with their instruments altogether and build jackets with electronic lapels that they would play instead. As Kraftwerk member Florian Schneider looked up to camera and leered maniacally, it was abundantly clear that The Kraftwerks, or whatever their name was, were a bizarre Teutonic novelty act of whom we would never hear again, lacking as they did both the charm and the durability of Rolf Harris and his Stylophone. The electronic lapels never appeared but Kraftwerk, the least rock 'n' roll of bands, went on to make a discreetly colossal impact, laying the foundations for techno, hip-hop and electro-pop among other genres, and their influence was keenly felt on both sides of the Atlantic. By 1986, their work – essentially, the electrification of modern pop music – was complete and they lapsed into semi-retirement, although they still spasmodically played live, including numbers performed on pocket calculators, as William Woollard noted retrospectively in the 1990. 'All very . . . numerical,' he concluded, quizzically.

'THE' PINK FLOYD

One of *Tomorrow's World*'s most significant interfaces with the world of rock music occurred in 1967 when a young psychedelic group from Cambridgeshire, then led by a wide-eyed youth named Syd Barrett, appeared on the show. However, the primary source of interest to *TW* was the lighting that had been laid on by Mike Leonard, an architect based in Highgate who had became landlord to the young band. The projector he set up, which used discs with coloured patterns pushed through optical devices, was intended to provide a light show that could be improvised in a musical fashion. Strictly secondary in the report were 'The Pink Floyd', whose purpose in the piece was to provide 'music with a range of unusual sounds' as accompaniment to the main attraction. Syd Barrett eventually became an acid casualty, leaving Pink Floyd then quitting music altogether to live a reclusive life in Cambridge. The rest of the band struggled on as best as they could without him, before eventually splitting up.

THE 'TEACH YOURSELF' COMPUTER ORGAN

In a *Tomorrow's World* retrospective, Maggie Philbin, wincing at the memory of Messrs Rodd and Prendiville's occasional forays into musical performance, announced her relief that she had never attempted to sing or play anything herself on the show. This, however, was not strictly true, for in demonstrating the 'Teach Yourself' computer organ – a simple enough device where a computer screen indicated where to plonk your fingers for the desired musical effect – she provided one of *TW*'s eerier moments. As she bashed merrily away like a Blackpool Wurlitzer virtuoso, she turned her head to camera and glowered enigmatically, in the manner of Sparks keyboardist Ron Mael, as if momentarily possessed. It was genuinely unsettling.

LEFT Maggie Philbin pays homage to Sparks

THE ADJUSTABLE FRETLESS BASS

The world of annoying bass guitar solos was turned upside-down when this item was demonstrated to the white-bearded Bob Symes in 1984, in the format of a quite enchanting piece of theatre. Old Bob approached his potting shed in a magnificent pair of red wellies, only for the door to be thrust open and, amid rising plumes of dry ice, a long-haired European of some description to emerge, thumb thwacking away at his fret bass. But then – and here came the truly wizardly bit – by turning a key, he lifted the frets and the bass became fretless! The spectacle left poor Bob frozen catatonic in his wellies. The fate of the adjustable fretless bass has been obscured in the dry-ice mists of time, but doubtless its inventor is in a shed somewhere, still thwacking away.

LEFT AND RIGHT The future of rock'n'roll . . . witnessed in a potting shed

BELOW The adjustable bass fretboard

THE SILENT DISCO

This was one for the twenty-something+ old folks. At the discotheque of tomorrow, reported Philippa Forrester, music would be pinpointed to certain zones of the dance floor, using ultrasonic methods. Step inside those zones and you could enjoy what the late Raymond Baxter would doubtless have described as 'some bangin' techno'. Step outside of them and you would hear nothing at all, enabling you to enjoy chat-up lines from lairy strangers in civilized quietude, rather than having them bawl, 'Do you come here often?' as they slobbered down your earlobe.

THE LOGICAL BASSOON

Ever since *Tomorrow's World*'s inception, the programme has been periodically vexed by one paramount musicological question: how can we devise a bassoon more in keeping with the 21st century? In 1967, Professor Giles Brindley felt he had the answer. An amateur bassoonist, he found that he was too busy a man to put in the hours of practice required to master the instrument's wide fingering span. He did, however, have the time to build a prototype 'logical' bassoon, wherein, by setting up a series of electrical connections, the keys could be more conveniently clustered. In 1990, a second inventor, Edgar Brown, devised a modern bassoon of his own, but his innovations were more acoustic than electronic-based. Finally, in 1997, *TW* decided to settle the matter once and for all with a run-off between the two rival instruments, with a trained contra-bassoonist trying out both. He gave the nod to Brown, since the Brindley bassoon, for all its logic, gave him backache when he tried to play it. Nevertheless, this was marvellous progress, and no doubt by the year 2040 we will see the first bassoon in outer space.

RIGHT A simpler, more sensible version of the old bassoon

THE COMPACT DISC

It's strange that something about which *TW* was so prescient remains so fixed in the minds of many as a supreme example of the show's naivety. The moment occurred in 1981. It was prefaced by a video clip of the Bee Gees performing their latest hit single, lined up and harmonising defiantly into an off-camera army of hairdryers, manes rampant. Then an unusually

earnest Kieran Prendiville explained that the Bee Gees' latest release would also be available in the much smaller, digital format of the compact disc. 'It's very similar to the video discs we've featured before,' he continued. Demonstrating how it was all done with lasers and so forth, he famously illustrated the format's indestructibility compared with vinyl by subjecting it to all manner of abuse, scrubbing and scratching at it (however, he didn't eat baked beans off it, as has been apocryphally reported). The only snag was that he was doing most of it to the disc's top – the side that carries no digital information. As we all know, the other side turned out to be rather more vulnerable: indeed, were a flake of skin to fall onto it from a gnat's kneecap, it would be enough to send your disc hopping about in your sound system like a bean on a hot plate. 'Whether there's a market for this disc remains to be seen,' an overly cautious Prendiville concluded.

LEFT 'Never Mind the Bee Gees, meet the Cee Dees!'

RIGHT AND BELOW Even after extreme coin abuse, CDs will never jump. Official!

TOMORROW'S
COMMUNICATION
TECHNOLOGY

HELLO?
I'M ON A
HOVERTRAIN

'Imagine,' Michael Blakstad wrote in his introduction to the 1979 book *Tomorrow's World Looks to the Eighties*, 'a world-wide network of telephones and television screens linked both to homes and to computers, making the communication of information and of visual images a flexible activity in which anyone can join.' This loose description of something like what eventually came to be known as the Internet is perhaps as close as *Tomorrow's World* ever got to predicting the emergence of the World Wide Web. James Burke came close too but, despite the fact that the Internet had been in use since the late 1960s in the military and among academics, and that the first email message was sent in 1969 (it was meant to read 'log' but the computer crashed midway through so it simply said 'lo'), the Internet managed to evade *TW*'s speculative grasp. Still, the developments that it did predict still have that wonderful antique whiff of lost futures about them – even if, sadly, many of them went a bit Clive Sinclair.

THE 'READYCALL' IN-CAR TELEPHONE SYSTEM

In 1971, tutted James Burke, the average senior businessman spent much of his important time in traffic between meetings, 'wasting about £20 an hour of the company's money'. No longer, however, thanks to the 'Readycall' system. With its extensive network of 360 subscribers and dedicated switchboard team of young ladies on standby, this in-car system enabled the stressed executive stuck in traffic to send such important messages as 'I'm stuck in traffic'. It represented the cutting edge in on-the-move telephone technology of the early 1970s, second only to the GPO radiophone, for which there was an impossibly long waiting list. Modest as the Readycall set-up was, once the director of postal communications, one John Edwards, gave it the go-ahead, it was the first system to divide the telephone network up into cells. This paved the way for today's widespread use of mobile phones. So you've Mr Edwards to thank, or thump, for that.

RIGHT 'Hello? I'm in a car'

LEFT 3-D junk mail. This, we probably will get

THE MICROWRITER

In 1981, *Tomorrow's World* declared that the microwriter, the invention of one Cy Enfield, was poised to render obsolete writing paper, the electric typewriter and even the word processor. It might have had the colouring of an under-brewed cup of tea, but this little brown, handheld beauty not only contained a microchip memory, but also enabled the user to dictate their thoughts at a speed much faster than conventional typing. This was all down to its six-button 'chording' keyboard, which enabled you to write letters of the alphabet by using learned key combinations. Despite the endorsement of Douglas Adams and, rather movingly, the testimony on *TW* of one Chris Channon, a cerebral palsy sufferer who was able to become a published journalist and poet thanks to the microwriter, for most people it all felt a bit too much like learning to play the piano for their liking. Production of the microwriter ceased in 1985. Shame.

72

LEFT The microwriter in fashionable beige

ABOVE RIGHT Mr Microwriter, Chris Channon

RIGHT 'Does it come in orange?'

THE WEARABLE COMPUTER

In 2000, a device was mooted that suited that doddery gadget-fiend and *TW* presenter Peter Snow right down to the ground: a mini-computer protuberance that you attached to the side of your spectacles. This enabled you to peruse a shopping list as you pottered up and down the aisles wondering what the devil you'd come in for, as well as housing a built-in program that spared the blushes of those who had trouble putting names to faces. By matching the data of the friendly fellow shaking your hand in front of you, on whom you'd obviously made a far stronger impression when you last met than vice versa, the mini-computer would scramble through its database and come up with his name. This belongs to the future, sadly, so for now, amnesiac old duffers will have to soldier on helplessly without cyborg assistance.

THE MOBILE-PHONE TIE

As modelled, once more, by a beaming Peter Snow, this slice of kipper neck-joy was mooted by a sanguine *TW* as the communications sensation of the next few decades. That fabric may be an unwise shade of grey but it is programmable! And that keyboard design is not just a piece of hideous whimsy but an actual, functioning pad, enabling you to dial numbers, for example, simply by twiddling at your tie in the manner popularised by the late Oliver Hardy. We were promised that this would be with us 'by 2005', yet a glimpse around Tie Rack mercifully tells us that this sartorial abomination has not yet come to pass.

THE TELECONFERENCING HEADSET

Tomorrow's World first predicted 'Confravision' back in the early 1970s. Then, in 2000, Philippa Forrester road-tested this elaborate contraption, ideal for the 21st-century executive who is forever in the back of a car in gridlock and late for that vital eleven o'clock with her team. Now, by donning the headset, which would fit neatly and conveniently into the average-sized suitcase, she could hook up with her colleagues by remote video. Could it be, however, that this will never catch on for the same reason as the videophones we all imagined we would be getting around about 1982 never did – that one of mankind's greatest pleasures is the reassurance that the person on the other end of the line is unable to know for certain where you are, what you're wearing, or doing, or scratching?

THE TELEMEDICINE SYSTEM

Tomorrow's World had predicted the 'computerised doctor' as far back as 1970 in the *TW* annual and this was one the programme stuck with and was eventually vindicated on. Today, ambulance personnel routinely use state-of-the-art communications technology to send forward data on emergency cases as they weave at high speed through traffic. However, modifications were required along the way. By 1981, a 'cardio-track' system existed, enabling a patient to transmit data as regards the condition of his heart to a specialist up in faraway Newcastle. However, the entire 'guinea pig's outhouse' look of the procedure was somewhat off-putting, with some viewers deciding they would rather risk a coronary than clamp a damn-fool thing like that to their nipples.

BELOW New telecommunications technology enables Judith Hann to converse with male nipple

THE OPTICAL COMPUTER

Back in 1974, engineers at the Radio Corporation of America were in the process of developing optical computers, using lasers to write, store and read holographic information on them. These binocular-style devices could, in theory, also be used to transmit messages via laser, offering a more secure channel of communication than radio. Unfortunately, as yet this device hasn't even had the chance not to catch on, since scientists still haven't managed to circumvent the basic snag that light-based transistors use up far more energy, and are a great deal more cumbersome, than regular transistors. And so it is that the use of lasers has generally been restricted to such mundane purposes as eye surgery, or threatening the testicles of British Secret Service agents.

THE SOUND SPECTACLES

This is nothing to do with Jean-Michel Jarre. In the early 1970s, *TW* heralded the arrival of a new aid for the blind. The spectacles contained three disks, just above the tip of the nose, between the lenses. These were traducers, radiating and receiving signals from a cone-shaped area covering a 60 degree arc in front of the wearer. Any obstacles in that range would bounce back 'echoes' which would pass down the cable behind the ear to an amplifier worn on the chest, then be rerouted to a tiny earpiece. This would enable the wearer to 'see' 20 feet in front of him. This bit of technology remains in development to this day, with no immediate prospect of guide dogs joining the canine equivalent of the dole queue.

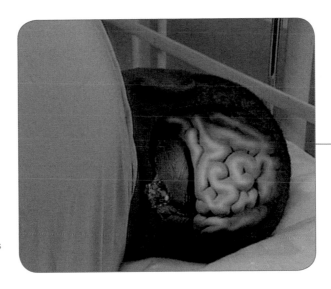

RIGHT Tomorrow's Brain – the chips are down

THE THOUGHT-READING COMPUTER

Casting its net of speculation decades into the future, *Tomorrow's World* floated the possibility at the turn of the millennium that, by attaching an interface chip to the base of the brain, it would be possible to transmit thoughts, albeit simple ones at first, directly onto a computer screen. This isn't quite as far-fetched as it sounds (well, OK, it's very nearly as far-fetched). There is, for example, a digital security group based in Canada that is currently working on the idea of 'pass thoughts' to replace passwords. Certainly, such a development would leave human fingers, no longer having to type thoughts, free for other tasks such as making mobile phone calls with their tie, scratching, and heavily editing and deleting the chaotic, neurological and even pornographic slush that would doubtless splat onto our screens if ever the technology were developed to lift the lid on our skulls.

TOMORROW'S HOUSEHOLD

INTELLIGENT KITCHENS AND OTHER DUMB IDEAS

Since the Industrial Revolution and the era of mechanisation, the history of the world has been a history of attempted labour-saving breakthroughs. It thus made perfect sense for *Tomorrow's World* to surmise that the dedicated scientists and patentees of today and  tomorrow would steadfastly continue that tradition. Although *TW* also hoped that the development of frictionless fabrics would preclude the need for cleaning the car, thus freeing up Sunday mornings to a great degree, they conceded that Mr and Mrs Great Britain, their 2.4 children and their dog would still be living in essentially the same sort of households as their ancestors and obliged to perform the same sorts of tasks, even with the supplementary assistance of a live-in robot. Hence, Britain's inventors exerted every sinew so that we wouldn't have to, creating ever more ingenious domestic contraptions to take the edge off our chores and make living in the future just that touch less onerous.

LEFT The future antidote to dirty phone calls? 'Take that, you pervert!'

RIGHT Michael Rodd talks manure

THE BALLBARROW

As gizmos went, it made sense. By replacing the traditional wheel with a sturdy plastic ball, the barrow would theoretically be more stable and easily manoeuvrable. One might imagine it flying out of the DIY stores. However, it is never hard to distinguish between a futurist and a frequent user of wheelbarrows. These hard-bitten, allotment-prowling folk do not hold with new-fangled innovations. They would rather struggle on with their old, spindly wheelies, even if it means accidentally tipping half a hundredweight of compost over their prized hollyhocks every now and again, than be seen dead or alive pushing around a contraption kept upright by some sort of beach ball ('They'll be putting jet packs on our barrows next!').

THE BAGLESS VACUUM CLEANER

The inventor of the Ballbarrow was, as it happens, James Dyson, who went on to invent the bagless vacuum cleaner. As far back as 1983, Kieran Prendiville was demonstrating its use of centrifugal force in picking up dust. However, Dyson encountered resistance from the industry, which was quite happy with the old, bagged cleaners. Only when Dyson licensed his cleaners in Japan in the 1990s did they take off, as Western shake 'n' vaccers decided that, while the industry might have been happy keeping quiet about new technology and flogging them ill-fitting Hoover bags ad infinitum, they were not.

Don't try this at home

Don't try this at home

THE UNDERWATER DRILL

In 1990, Michael Rodd demonstrated, with the assistance of inventor Vic Brown, a means whereby, if you were of a mind to, you could wield your Black & Decker under water and sidestep the customary nuisance of being fatally electrocuted while doing so. The trick was to spray the drill, and, of course, the plug, as Mr Rodd had urgently to be reminded by Mr Brown, with an aerosol can of 'water inhibitor'. This disabled the electric shock-giving properties of the drill, enabling the DIY enthusiast to get on with those submarine chores he imagined he would never be able to tackle. As Mr Brown plunged his drill into a tank of water, a neon blue banner urged viewers 'Don't try this at home', though one wonders if viewers of a mind to do so would have the basic literacy skills to understand the message.

Mr Brown survived the demonstration, and one might have mistaken Michael Rodd's expression for one of mild chagrin. 'Do it again,' he bade Mr Brown, as if in the subconscious hope that this time ... But the 'water inhibitor' spray did its job once more. Mysteriously, the public failed to see the benefits of underwater drilling and its myriad possibilities. Perhaps its time has yet to come; when the global warming predicted by *Tomorrow's World* in the 1980s does its stuff and entire cities are submerged, then Vic Brown will at last be onto a winner.

THE STEPS-CUM-IRONING BOARD

We've all been in that pesky situation. You want to fetch that bound volume of *The World's Greatest Seafaring Odysseys* from the top shelf, but you've some urgent ironing to do at the same time. You need steps and you need an ironing board and you need them pretty damn simultaneously. Thank heavens, then, for the steps-cum-ironing board! Once you have reached down your precious tome, you simply descend, convert your steps and at once attend to running a crease over your jeans without a second having been wasted.

THE HOT PAINT

In the late 1960s the Pain Research Laboratories invented an electrically conductive, graphite-based paint. Once a wall was painted, the whole surface could be plugged into a power source. Say goodbye to the humble radiator, that quaint relic of the mid-20th century! A lick of this could even solve the problem of icy roads. Sadly, the trail ran cold on hot paints, so they invented hot pants instead.

THE JUMPER WRAPPER

Kindly, bearded old codger Bob Symes was not the sort of *TW* presenter who imparted the sense that, one day, cybernauts would be our valets and schoolchildren's satchels would be convertible into jet packs so that they could make it to assembly in time. For sheer olde worlde modesty, his 'jumper wrapper' took the biscuit. An elaborate wooden device that sat in the corner like a semi-retired occasional table, the 'jumper wrapper' was designed, in about 1876 by the look of it, to put an end to the centuries-old drudgery of manually folding and putting away your woolly jumpers. Now, as Symes calmly demonstrated, it was a matter of a few minutes and a black belt in the woollens equivalent of origami simply to fold your jumper around the wooden device, up, round and between its elaborate slats and school desk-type lid, and your knitwear would be fresh and ready for your next trip to the local branch of the Sea Shanty Appreciation Society.

LEFT No sense of ironing? Not now. Converted at a moment's notice. . . and fold away. And throw away

RIGHT Wool origami – the Jumper Wrapper

THE MICROWAVEABLE HOT-WATER BOTTLE

This was a cracker. It wasn't a bottle. It wasn't filled with water. But it *was* red and it was certainly hot, thanks to a short spell in the microwave. This was where the microchip served the needs of those for whom even central heating was not enough to warm their little extremities under the duvet. 'Hotties' and similar derivations of this device are widely available, but they do lack the authentic touch of accidentally scalding yourself with boiling water from the kettle as you shakily attempt to pour it into a good old-fashioned like-mother-used-to-fill-them rubber bottle.

THE VACUUM HAIRCUT

As co-demonstrated by Howard Stableford in 1992, this involved an exciting new synergy between state-of-the-art coiffure and vacuum cleaning. The wheeze was that, by attaching different lengths of tube to the cleaner, you would enable the hairdresser (even a female hairdresser)

LEFT The vacuum haircut – it both sucked and blowed

more easily to cut the hair of the customer to different lengths – short at the sides, long at the top, or even the other way round, as was the style in 1992. A shame really, that they didn't think to develop a vacuum cleaner that would suck up in their entirety any human being who would consider wearing a mullet.

THE RUBBER PLANT-CUM-TV AERIAL

This innovation represented an astonishing feat of synergy between interior decor and high-quality picture reception. Simply wire up this amazing device to your rubber plant and you could simultaneously enjoy both your fake foliage and an on-screen blizzard purporting to represent *Home and Away* on five.

THE AUTOMATIC ROTARY FINGER CLEANER

'A rotary action will ensure the removal of even the most ingrained dirt,' the *TW* presenter assured us, or at least assured us that the inventors of the device had assured him. A sort of pencil sharpener for people with dirty fingernails, one suspected from the barely suppressed smirks of the presenter that he realised that this extraneous, faintly lewd little gizmo was not likely to be the stuff of which the 21t century would be made.

THE PERFUMED DOG COLLAR

The idea of this indispensable accessory, as Judith Hann patiently explained, was that each time an agitated canine barked, the woof would trigger off a mechanism that released a pleasant scent, appeasing the yapping hound and causing its baying to abate. There was something inherently churlish about this device to the dog-loving British mentality, however: take away a dog's bark and you are taking away a part of its character, its soul. You might as well try to invent an anti-tail-wagging mechanism.

THE INTELLIGENT KITCHEN

In 2000, *TW*'s Philippa Forrester predicted, with working models, what the kitchen of the immediate future would look like. Essentially, our role would be reduced to one of onlookers, thereby increasing our leisure time still further. Scrabbling about in an old drawer for that dog-eared, greasy-paged copy of *Mrs Beeton's Book of Household Management*? No longer – the fridge of the future would feed us with recipes, drawn from a database of its own contents! As for the bins, well, far from being smelly, perpetually overfilled items in the corner, they would become the technological hub of the entire kitchen operation. As you dumped your rubbish in them, your bin would sort the contents into the appropriate compartments for recycling, using almost enough electric energy in doing so to carbon-justify the operation, one presumes. Furthermore, the 'super-bin' would take note of the packaging you had thrown out and send an email to the microwave, which would then top up the relevant items, buying them over the Internet. All of this, promised Philippa and the gang, would be in place 'by 2005'. Hmm. As I regard my own kitchen, its fridge containing a jar of mustard empty save for a furry green lining, and the swing bin boasting a three-week-old teabag barnacled to its side, 2005 seems a long, long way away.

THE FOLDAWAY CHOPPING BOARD

'My kitchen looks like a battlefield after dinner parties – chopped vegetables everywhere!' trilled *TW* presenter Kate Bellingham in 1991, leading many military historians to suspect that she was labouring under a misapprehension about actual battlefield conditions, in which diced aubergines do not greatly feature. She was

demonstrating the 'foldaway chopping board' which, when adjusted, turned itself into a chute down which carrots and courgettes could neatly slide without spilling hither and yon, resulting in scenes reminiscent of the Napoleonic Wars. It wasn't a half-bad idea, as it happened, and was the invention of one Mark Sanders, who shot to initial fame in the 1980s as the inventor of a foldaway bike, the progress of which was halted by the late-1980s recession. Sanders persevered however, not just with the bike but also with a number of other devices, including a foldaway surgeon's table. Decades ago, when asked what the future would be about, as others spoke of condos on Mars or electronically dispensed toilet roll, only one man had the vision to stand up and say 'folding'. And he was right.

THE PORTABLE DOG KENNEL

After the 20th century and Laika, the first dog in space, *TW* pondered the big question: What will life be like for Tomorrow's Dog? It offered two suggestions. The first was another miracle of foldaway technology: the Go-Anywhere Kennel. This was exhibited in 1992 and was pretty much self-descriptive: those for whom convenience was no object when it came to having their faithful pooches travel with them wherever they went, could carry the kennel about manually, in flat-pack form, before instantly converting on impact with the ground into a wooden shelter for Fido. It would be fair to say that the Go-Anywhere Kennel has not turned out to be the technological sensation of the age.

LEFT Funnel vision – the foldaway chopping board

RIGHT Preposterous pooch pampering – the 'Go-Anywhere Kennel'

KIERAN PRENDIVILLE

Having started television life as one of the bright young minions on Esther Rantzen's Sunday evening consumer-affairs show *That's Life*, drolly recounting what the Electricity Board said when he rang them, Kieran Prendiville transferred to *Tomorrow's World*, where he soon established a jauntier, more detached attitude to some of the ill-conceived tat he was asked to present as the stuff of the future. He was the man who introduced post-modern irony to the show in floppy-haired dollops, given licence to jest as the 1980s dawned and it become clear that the Supersonic Era of Progress was taking a bit of a nosedive. If a bubble car running on past-its-sell-by-date cabbage was rubbish, Prendiville didn't wait for posterity's verdict: he said so. Comedy was clearly his forte, and it was in that capacity as a writer that he made his post-*TW* career in the 1990s.

MAGGIE PHILBIN

Maggie Philbin's career at *Tomorrow's World* spanned eight years, and so strong an impression did she make on the viewers, particularly those of the adolescent male variety, that her many other achievements have been overshadowed. She studied drama at Manchester University, alongside future luminaries of *The Young Ones* Adrian Edmondson, Rik Mayall and Ben Elton, before going on to join *The Multi-Coloured Swap Shop*, during which time she married Keith 'Cheggers' Chegwin. As half of Brown Sauce, she even had a 1981 no. 15 hit single with Noel Edmonds, 'I Wanna Be a Winner', which sadly receives infrequent airplay nowadays. However, it was when she was introduced to add further oestrogen to *Tomorrow's World* that she really made her mark. Her general demeanour of wide-eyed, elfin credulity enabled her to get through studio demonstrations such as that of the cagoule that converted into an emergency inflatable tent without even a hint of scepticism. Her Worm Omelette moment came during an item in which, in the name of science and teasing the female presenters, she was forced to confront her fear of snakes. She wasn't quite as unflappable as Michael Rodd (indeed, she flapped more than somewhat) but the snake she was presented with seemed even more frightened of her, rapidly disappearing up a chimney. Philbin continues to present regularly on a range of science issues, mainly on BBC news programmes.

BOB SYMES

Bob Symes is one of the forgotten men of *Tomorrow's World*, but he was a fondly remembered fixture of the show during the 1980s, when he tended to present self-contained, out-in-the-field items. With his ruddy countenance and the sense that he was a hard man to coax out of his potting shed for his evening meals, he had about him the air of *The Fast Show*'s Coughing Bob Fleming, though thankfully minus the coughing. Of Austrian, aristocratic descent, his full name is Robert Alexander Baron Schutzmann von Schutzmansdorff, but we can call him Bob. An inventor, he had managed to lose parts of several fingers while devising contraptions in his shed, but *TW* camera directors artfully kept his damaged digits away from our screens. It was hard, on the face of it, to think of a person worse suited to *TW* than Symes, a Santa-bearded model railway enthusiast to whom you suspect it remains news that there is such a thing as the Internet. However, there was something reassuring about his pottering presence, as if to suggest that the future wasn't just for the young 'uns. Today he concentrates his efforts on attempting to reopen disused railway lines, but found time in 2007 to marry Dr Sheila Gunn, the works manager at Boston Lodge on the Ffestiniog Railway.

TOMORROW'S ROBOTS

CYBER NOUGHTIES

One of the first robots to feature on *Tomorrow's World* was 'Able Mabel', designed by the magnificently named Professor Meredith Thring in 1966. 'Begin your day with Able Mabel,' trilled the voiceover. 'She'll run your bath to the exact temperature she knows you'll like, she'll make your bed and lay out your clothes for another day, free from household drudgery, free from time-wasting chores like vacuum cleaning.' Able Mabel, however, was not so much an existing metal entity as a hopeful projection, a twinkle in Professor Thring's eye. It was ever thus with *Tomorrow's World*: long on optimism about robots, short on actual robots who could walk the walk. Still, *TW* never wavered in its faith and hope that the future, albeit one constantly postponed, will see mankind coexisting with helpful metal chums built in its own image, or at least in the image of its waste-paper bins.

LEFT Inspired by Hissing Sid, Kieran Prendiville invents the robo dance

THE ROBOT BARMAID

Cynthia, the robot barmaid programmed to mix 75 cocktails, appeared on *Tomorrow's World* going head-to-head with a human barkeep. Philippa Forrester was to judge whether a James Bond Martini tasted better shaken by the barman or, since robots apparently cannot shake, stirred by Cynthia. In the end, Forrester couldn't tell the difference between either. However, with the supply of young Australians showing no sign of giving out, there is no reason to believe that automatons will be attending to our imbibing needs in the immediate future. As for Cynthia, she lent her name to a South London nightclub that was purchased by two infamous denizens of the fetish scene, Brian and Caroline Sheridan. They changed the name of the club but Cynthia still mixes drinks for its clients, while presumably keeping a wary eye out for patrons with a thing for inanimate objects.

THE MOWBOT

For a mere £400 in 1970, a US company was vending an automatic lawnmower. You sank a thin cable around the outer edge of the lawn and plugged the two ends into a small transmitter, which sent an electrical signal around the cable. The battery-operated mower would then move about at random across the lawn but, thanks to inbuilt sensors, turn away from the cable on picking up the electrical signal. It even had back-up sensors in case the first set of sensors failed, preventing the robot from going over the cable on a chomping rampage across the flowerbeds. Mowbots have remained on the market to this day, but they're not cheap. You might well be advised to check both the size of your bank balance and your backside to see if this particular labour-saving purchase is really advisable.

THE ROBO-RODEO

In 1978, Judith Hann was dispatched to the southern states of America, amid the rooting-tooting, muscle-bound cowpunchers of the rodeo scene. What with the popularity of the sport, it had been deemed necessary to devise a mechanical rodeo simulator. As a visibly anxious, cowboy hat-sporting Hann levered herself into the saddle, a good ol' boy threw the switch and the simulator began rocking and reeling, with Hann just about holding on both to the saddle and her essential Judith Hann-ness. Mechanical rodeo simulators rock on to this day. *TW* was bang on the money with this one, although in 1978 they might well have been surprised at that.

THE ROBOT SHEEP-SHEARER

The first time a sheep was sheared robotically was in Australia in 1979. By 1984 the practice was going strong and so Kieran Prendiville was sent Down Under to see how it all worked. With the sheep looking on as anxiously as cows fearing the cold hand of the milkmaid, Prendiville explained how the kit worked. The 'robot' was able to perform the delicate task of shearing thanks to a computer programme in which were stored thousands of measurements, enabling it to cope with the varying shapes and contours of any sheep that came into its clasp. We were assured that the sheep did not endure any more pain than they would with the average brawny farmhand, but looking at the sheep themselves, like some real-life recreations of a Nick Park animation, upside-down and legs splayed apart, it was hard to contemplate wearing a woolly jumper with a clear conscience ever again. Robot sheep-shearing continued to develop into the early 1990s until the Australian wool industry was beset by a financial crisis which precluded any further significant investment in the technology. So, for the time being, it's back to the big fellers with the clippers.

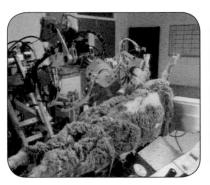

THE ROBOT APPLE-HARVESTER

Human beings, especially those of the penurious variety, of whom there is always a plentiful supply, had always been considered the most effective apple-pickers. However, in 1992, *TW* introduced us to the robot apple-harvester. It worked by shooting out an arm in a straight line, stopping when

a sensor told it that it had hit an apple, then gripping the fruit and depositing it in a basket with ruthless efficiency. There was no Hissing about with this machine; it was a veritable Terminator of the orchard, a cruel, rustic spoiler. The Belgians are very keen on it, apparently.

THE ADVANCED PERSONAL ROBOT

The R-1000 resembled a miniature swing bin and was painted in colours that even a subservient automaton should not have to endure. Nevertheless, Philippa Forrester assured us that there was more to this little chap than trundling around on castors looking cute. *TW* touted the

R-1000, developed in Japan, as the first advanced personal robot, a technological harbinger of a day to come when robots would be cheerfully sorting our laundry, vacuuming, even gardening. That said, on demonstration the R-1000 didn't appear to have much of a knack for skivvying. It was capable of recognising faces, for all the good that would do around the house,

as well as storing and speaking recorded messages. The long and the short of it is that we're going to be sorting our own smalls for a good while yet.

THE ROBOT TUNA

For those who were wondering for years why we could put a man on the moon but we couldn't invent a robot tuna, the retort came in the 1990s via Carol Vorderman on *Tomorrow's World*. The robot tuna was designed precisely to replicate the make-up of an actual tuna, from top to tailfin, lacking only the fish's brain, though with the greatest of respect to the piscine, that is probably no great loss. The robot tuna tastes lousy in brine and it is, of course, a great shame about the robot dolphins that get caught up in the robot tuna nets. However, the purpose of this ersatz mechanical creature, as well as to loosen the teeth of a few unsuspecting sharks, is advanced undersea exploration. Once scientists get around the slight problem of waterproofing, an ocean-going robot tuna should be in operation any time soon.

ABOVE the surprisingly effective robo apple-picker

LEFT Go on son, kick it!

RIGHT straight-faced Carol Vorderman introduces the robo tuna

THE FAMOUS 'HISSING SID' FIASCO

It was all nicely set up. A waistcoat-sporting Kieran Prendiville stared thoughtfully at the green baize as the Voice of Snooker himself, Ted Lowe, did a live commentary in those familiar, hushed tones. Cut to Prendiville's opponent, a robot developed by the University of Reading's cybernetics department named 'Hissing Sid', a reference to the 1980 novelty hit 'Captain Beaky' with which the nation had become weak-mindedly besotted. It was Hissing Sid's turn at the table. However, the robot froze. Even Ted Lowe was struggling to improvise behind the microphone. 'And . . . any minute . . . it will happen.' Except it didn't. A nervous hand shot out from off-camera and made some sort of adjustment that reanimated Hissing Sid. He jerked into action, levering a two-way cue and lining up behind a hand-placed white ball. Sid played his shot – missing a red ball that was poised so close to the pocket that a sneeze would have put it in.

In later demonstrations, Hissing Sid could be seen in all his glory. Ostensibly an example of the leading edge of Artificial Intelligence, he actually looked like he'd been bashed together from the contents of a skip. For his next trick, he failed to pick up a large plate using a suction pad as Prendiville looked on with both mock and genuine exasperation. Finally, Sid attempted to dress a salad, but instead spilt the vinaigrette several inches outside the bowl. If Hissing Sid did achieve anything prior to being broken up for scrap, it was to allay any popular dystopian fears that science had overstretched itself and that robots were on the verge of becoming our masters.

ABOVE Hissing
Sid cocks up
the red

RIGHT Hissing Sid
applies snooker
skills to salad
dressing

PILLS
GRILLS AND
BELLYACHING

This category is in no sense a shabby attempt to avoid using the sweep-up category of 'miscellaneous' for, as James Burke would doubtless point out, there are strong connections between these three, seemingly disparate categories. We need buildings in which to live and work, 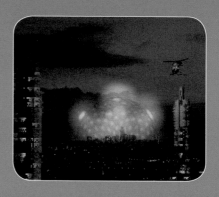 these buildings need to be secure, and in order to live in these secure buildings we need food to survive. So there you have it. *TW* may in its time have differed from its sometime patron Prince Charles, who regarded modern buildings as 'carbuncles'; sadly, time seems to have been on HRH's side. They were on more solid ground with security, most of their predictions having come into play in some form or other, though not necessarily in the ways they had in mind. As for food, well, very early on in the programme's history, in 1966, Raymond Baxter vaguely suggested that food would be replaced by special pills, which would certainly cut down on the whole Number Two problem. More accurate was its suggestion of synthetic foods, as those who have ever tasted Quorn – vegetarian cuisine's answer to the pencil eraser – will testify.

ABOVE Huge artificial lights keep city working in future - global warming no longer an issue, apparently

RIGHT Where the cyber-Brents shall toil – the office of the future and its 'state of the art' air con system

THE OFFICE BUILDING OF THE FUTURE

In 1972, reported *Tomorrow's World*, the Greater London Council opened a new office block on a roundabout just off Addington Street, close to Westminster. Known as the 'island block', it was the very latest in open-plan office design. Over a serene, low-level ambient soundtrack gently thrumming like a perfectly functioning air-conditioning system, the *TW* narrator sang the praises of its sealed windows, scientifically controlled climate and state-of-the-art light, heat and ventilating systems. The whole thing might have looked like a storage facility for nuclear waste and come at a cost of £4m (and this in the 1970s) but this was, without doubt, the office building of the future. Unfortunately, in the immediate actual future, problems quickly arose. The blinds, designed to come down automatically when the sun came out, failed to go back up when the sun went back in. And so, on already dismal days, large sections of the office were plunged into semi-darkness. Furthermore, the air-conditioning system swept in the wind coming off the Thames, causing those in the south office to complain of the freezing cold and ask for the central heating to be turned up, which then created furnace-like conditions in the north office. The building might have survived but for the government abolishing the GLC in 1986. It shut down for good in 1990, an unloved relic of what-might-have-been for office luxury Jacques Tati-style.

THE BENDING SKYSCRAPERS

Once a decade, *Tomorrow's World* dropped in on a British school, harvesting the kids' take on possible future technological developments. In 1977, Michael Rodd visited Lewes Priory Comprehensive School. Its pupils came up with a number of intriguing proposals, one of which was a creature that was part-hen, part-cow. Known as a 'how', the hybrid would advantageously produce both milk and eggs. Yet more mind-boggling was the proposal of one teenage girl for bending skyscrapers. This unprecedented feat of architectural flexibility was devised solely with the convenience of the window cleaner in mind. Instead of him being forced to winch up the side of the building, the building would bend to him, like the mountain to Muhammad. As terrified 34th-floor office workers went flying, along with all their fixtures and fittings, typewriters and filing cabinets, they would know that their extensive injuries would be worth it for the extra gleam they would get on their panes. 'So, there you have it,' concluded Mr Rodd to camera. 'These children, the children to whom tomorrow's world belongs, are complete idiots. Heaven help us all.' In fact, he didn't say that, and one can be almost certain he didn't even think it.

THE POCKET-SIZED LASER GUN

In 1969, James Burke donned an outsize sombrero and ventured out onto the dusty American plains to demonstrate the potency of a new hand-held firearm that knocked the traditional revolver into a cocked hat. Taking out a blameless cactus in the middle distance with a single shot, Burke drew attention to the pulse argon laser, which accounted for the gun's potency. Right now, it was a little cumbersome – about the size of a small telescope. However, said Burke, scientists were working on a significantly smaller model, 'Something maybe the ladies can slip into their handbags', a remark that managed to be mildly sexist and empowering to women at the same time. It was the 1960s. Everyone was confused. Sadly, the laser gun never made it into domestic use and the womenfolk had to make do with mace.

THE SECURITY BRIEFCASE

In 1966, when London swang, beer was two bob a pint and you could buy a mews house in Kensington and still have change from a hundred guineas, Britain was riding high on a crest of the new-fangled. And nothing was fangled newer than the Security Briefcase, showcased that year on *TW* in a demonstration involving a city gent and two unconvincing footpads. Having wrested the case from the gent, the two rogues were flummoxed when it spontaneously sprouted three enormous metal limbs, converting itself into an unwieldy tripod and leaving them looking like proper, perishing berks. A dozen objections as to the feasibility of this device spring to mind, any one of which could have accounted for its demise. But, for a fleeting moment in 1966, we gave those confounded briefcase thieves a scare they wouldn't soon forget.

LEFT Convincing street tough confounded by the Security Briefcase

LEFT *TW* comedy
burglar has nation
in stitches

RIGHT Don't be
alarmed – it was
the Eighties

THE VANDAL-PROOF DOOR

Featuring presenter Peter Macann performing a mock break-in, sporting
a highly burglarious hooped jersey, the vandal-proof door item was classic
1970s *Tomorrow's World* fare. However sturdy a conventional lock, it is no
match for the determined thief armed with a sledgehammer. However,
this new door, developed by a security company in Buckinghamshire and
containing a lock that controlled a 3-foot bar, was impossible to break in.
Unfortunately, however, as a subsequent *Crime Monthly* item made clear,
the vandal-proof door was also copper-proof. As they televised a raid on
a suspected drugs den in South London, police found that even with their
beefiest chap on the job, they couldn't break down the door. Another
success story, then, for a *TW*-promoted item, and it was heartening to
know that the show's popularity spread even to the criminal *demi-monde*.

THE STATE-OF-THE-ART BURGLAR ALARM

In 1984, as society crumbled, its fabric torn apart by the effects of monetarism, the miner's strike and the lewdness of Frankie Goes To Hollywood, domestic security became a paramount concern. And so, Judith Hann introduced the very latest in anti-burglar technology. Away with the crude tintinnabulations of the traditional bell: instead, a 'voice chip', on prompting, would raise a vocoderized alarm. So, if an intruder should break and enter, the state-of-the-art burglar alarm would automatically sound out: 'Help. Help. Intruder. Intruder.' If there were a fire, it would let you know: 'Fire. Fire. Fire. Fire.' It would even inform you if you had left a window marginally open, or failed to configure the alarm system properly. Systems like this are currently available in the US for a worryingly inexpensive $82.95.

THE SAFETY WATER CUSHION

According to *Tomorrow's World* in 1974, the Americans were in the process of trying out a measure to prevent serious damage in car crashes – covering crash barriers with water-filled cushions made from heavy-duty plastic. These could be topped up via removable stoppers, which themselves would be forcibly ejected on impact with a car as a result of the compressive forces. It was also suggested that smaller versions of the cushions could be attached to the bumpers of cars and buses. The potential fun that could have been had with these would have made it worthwhile for those of a certain mentality actually to engineer car crashes. However, they went and invented boring old airbags instead.

THE 'GOOD GRACIOUS ALIVE' MOMENT

It was 1969, the year man first landed on the moon. That giant leap Raymond Baxter had observed with stoical equanimity – a small step, really, in mankind's inexorable progress. However, one item caused him to ejaculate verbally in a manner that was, in its own way, even more shocking than when Kenneth Tynan had infamously uttered the 'f' word on TV four years earlier. It happened as he watched a demonstration, heavily flanked by sandbags, of the effect two ounces of explosives could have on a sheet of reinforced metal. Following the detonation, Baxter crept out from his crouch position and inspected the near-perfect circular piece of metal the explosion had punched out. It was then that he uttered the immortal words, 'Goodness gracious alive', giving vent to emotions he had hitherto managed suavely to suppress. Why it should have been this incident in particular – a useful means, perhaps, of manufacturing steel frisbees. but no more – is unclear, but it undoubtedly exercised Baxter strangely. Sadly, like many things on *TW*, the expression never caught on.

LEFT 'Good gracious alive!' Baxter outburst stuns nation

RIGHT The worm omelette. The word rhymes with 'Yuck'

THE WORM OMELETTE

The earthworm, it turns out, writhing, brown and repulsive as it may be, is one of nature's most industrious little troupers. Because it thrives in animal waste, the worm is both an excellent recycler and a fine source of protein – so much so that, as a reward for its efforts, farmers were once looking to have it converted into animal food. In

1981, Michael Rodd decided there was no reason why animals should have all the gastronomic fun and so, in the spirit of wholly unnecessary research, decided that he should rustle up a worm omelette for himself. It has to be said for Rodd that, as the only-recently-deceased earthworms nestled in the pan, he did not for a second flinch, even as he brought the fork to his lips. He masticated pensively, as if testing out a new strain of wild mushroom, before a curt nod and a 'very interesting'. It may be that as the cameras cut away he charged offstage screaming for a minion to fetch a spittoon and a soda siphon, but you suspect he is made of firmer fibre than that.

THE CENTRIFUGAL INSTANT-COFFEE TRAY

John Clayton is the sort of fellow who, like Lymeswold cheese, is produced exclusively by England. He is an inventor and a dabbler in gadgets whose creations include a lamp made of an old saxophone and an ocular contraption designed to help him win Spot the Ball competitions (the secret of which, for obvious reasons, he jealously guards). He was also inspired by a *TW* item featuring Judith Hann in 1980: a tray for carrying three champagne glasses at once that, thanks to the principle of centrifugal force, swung but didn't spill. A small light bulb sparked in Mr Clayton's head to match the one in his saxophone. *TW* followed the various modifications in his quest for the perfect workplace tray on which to carry his plastic

beakers of coffee from the dispensing machine back to his desk. After various adjustments to the string length, and the breakthrough decision to opt for a metal base, he finally invented a pendulous device capable of carrying four cups of coffee at once. His achievement was rewarded by an almost touching tribute from his boss, who saw John carrying his centrifugal coffee-tray along the office corridor, and fleetingly considered asking him to make one for him. 'But then the thought went out of my head, and that was that,' he added. Talk about wildfire.

THE EDIBLE PETROLEUM SOLUTION

Tomorrow's World mooted this in their 1970 annual, in a feature entitled 'How to Eat Petrol and Thrive', which suggested a mouth-watering array of meat substitutes in the offing. They explained how, in order to combat food shortages, scientists were looking at ways of extracting the proteins derived from food from a variety of sources, including soya beans, carbohydrates and petroleum. In the late 1950s, a microbiological research team based in Marseilles discovered that animals (well, microbes) were quite happy to eat the waxes in petroleum products that freeze in cold weather. They then made it their task to see how they could develop this principle and thus introduce the protein element of petroleum into the human diet. However, BP, who commissioned the research, concluded in their report that the prospects of their customers agreeing to eat their product were remote. The only challenge to this scepticism so far provided by the 21st century is the true story of a man who, each night on the way home from work, would visit his local garage, imbibe a swift half-pint of petrol from the pump, pay for it, then be on his way.

THE SILENT BEANS

In 1984, according to Kieran Prendiville in a special *Tomorrow's World* item, the British were eating beans at the rate of two million tins a day. The gaseous emissions this was causing would not have assuaged emergent fears about the greenhouse effect. Of more immediate concern, however, was the social embarrassment. It seems that beans contain certain molecules that the body cannot break down. When these eventually run into the rather seedy bacteria that dwell in the lower intestine, gases are produced and noxious wind is duly broken. However, it was believed that by exposing beans to radiation, the offending molecules could be broken down into more digestible particles. And so, in the 1990s, *TW* looked in on one Colin Leakey, one of the Cambridge Leakeys, who is a world authority on beans and has devoted a perturbing amount of his life to seeking out an end to bean-induced flatulence. His studies took in NASA, who harboured serious concerns about the effects of baked bean consumption on astronauts (the suggestion 'Just don't give them any!' appears not to have featured in consultation papers), but eventually, his studies took him to southern Chile, where he discovered a bean known to natives for years whose effects are remarkably windless. Thus boosted, his work continues: a fart-free future could be within our grasp.

ABOVE LEFT Judith Hann about to get centrifugal

LEFT Beanz Meanz Flatulence? No more

PHILIPPA FORRESTER

Philippa Forrester began her career in children's TV, has worked on *Robot Wars*, *The Heaven and Earth Show* and *Barking Mad*, but it's her role as presenter on *Tomorrow's World* during the 1990s that remains the jewel in her broadcasting CV. Forrester was always an able presenter, comfortable in the smart, ultra-modern surroundings of 1990s *TW* and, like many of her *TW* colleagues, never guilty of overestimating the intelligence of her viewing public. She presented with some aplomb coverage of the total solar eclipse in August 1999. Since the demise of *TW*, Forrester has turned her attention to conservation, supporting campaigns encouraging home composting, and our dumb chums in the animal kingdom, in particular a young otter called Grace, around which she produced a documentary in 2007. In 2008, she co-presented *World on the Move* with Brett Westwood, a Radio 4 series about the migrating habits of animals. Her ardent environmentalism dates back to her *TW* days – while presenting the show, she was also taking a degree in ecology and conservation at Birkbeck College, University of London. This isn't incompatible – after all, today's recycled tin cans are tomorrow's robots, whether of the warring or domestic help variety.

PETER SNOW

An Oxford graduate and grandson of a First World War military man, General Thomas d'Oyly Snow, Peter Snow started life working on *ITN News*. He remains most famous for gesticulating wildly around swing-o-meter graphics on election nights, or presenting re-enactments of key moments of the Gulf Wars in sandboxes, but Peter Snow effectively brought to bear his twin qualities of certifiable braininess and overheated enthusiasm for all things tech-y on *Tomorrow's World* in its twilight years. For Snow, no device was too far-out and no prediction too outlandish, even if the details could be a little vague. He once predicted, for example, that scientists were on the verge of discovering a means to control extreme climate in America by coating the ocean in a special, molecular-thin substance. There was just one minor detail; 'They haven't found the right material yet.' There, alas, might be the snag. Today, Peter Snow hooks up with his son Dan, very much a chip off the old block, to present *21st Century Battlefields* for the BBC. He has decided, however, to step down from his gesticulating duties at the next General Election.

KENNETH WILLIAMS

On 3 December 1980, Kenneth Williams wrote in his diary: 'Went to BBC Centre for *Tomorrow's World* and it was a hell of a day: beginning with exercises in tracksuits on apparatus, then the dinner table scene and the eating of synthetic foods, and then me demonstrating the watch which gets its energy from body heat on the wrist.' However taxing this might have been, if anything he threw himself into his unlikely (and brief) role as *TW* presenter with a little too much gusto. If *TW*'s producers were looking for a hint of camp, he gave them a bucketful, purring nasally to camera about all the 'micro-ampules' running up and down his arm from the wristwatch. Although still alive, you sensed Raymond Baxter turning in his grave at all of this. Perhaps it was Williams's way of showing contempt. Just two days after his *TW* entry, he wrote in his diary: 'Apart from the news, the television isn't worth the licence money and I'm very glad I haven't got a set.' He died in 1988.

AND THOSE WHO ALSO SERVED ...

ANNA FORD

Briefly a presenter in the late 1970s, demonstrating devices such as a pair of precarious-looking dinghy-skis to enable easy pedestrian passage across shallow rivers, Ford resigned from the show stating that she did not wish to become a 'public figure'. Shortly after this, she joined *News at Ten*.

ADAM HART-DAVIS

Although most famous for telling us to pay our taxes and explaining what the Romans did for us, Hart-Davis also briefly told us what, in addition to more tax bills, we could expect in the future: he co-presented *TW* after the Millennium.

HOWARD STABLEFORD

A long-time, versatile and capable presenter of *Tomorrow's World* from 1985 onwards, Stableford ought to be better remembered than he actually is. But by this time, the show was on its slow decline towards becoming All Our Yesterdays.

CAROL VORDERMAN

Vorderman briefly took time out from *Countdown* to host *TW* in the 1990s, presenting items on spider silk and the robot tuna, among others, before a contractual dispute (connected to her appearing in a TV advert) led to her leaving the show.

DIARY OF THE FUTURE

In the *Tomorrow's World* Annual of 1970, James Burke presented his prognostications in the form of an almanac. Did he mean us?

1973

'One thousand dead in jumbo-jet collision over urban area.'
In 1977, two jumbo jets collided in Tenerife but it happened on the runway. There were 582 people killed, the highest figure for any aviation disaster.

1974

'Space shuttle launched.'
Optimistic – the first space shuttle made its maiden voyage in 1981.
'Automatic spacecraft orbits Jupiter and identifies red spot as ferrous cloud.'
Voyager first sent back detailed pictures of Jupiter's red spot in 1979. To this day, no one is certain why it's that colour. Burke's guess is as good as any.

1976

'Automatic spacecraft lands on Mars and finds a form of life.'
In 1996, NASA scientists in Houston reported the existence of fossil nano-organisms in a 4,500-million-year-old Martian meteorite that crashed to Earth in Antarctica about 13,000 years ago. In 2003, a consortium led by Professor Colin Pillinger launched *Beagle 2* in the general direction of Mars. No one knows what became of it.

1979

'Birth-control pill for man perfected.'
The male birth-control pill has been hailed as 'imminent' for many years now. However, its reported side-effects mean that most men have displayed a markedly low enthusiasm count when it comes to taking it up.
'Total control of obesity with drugs.'
Despite numerous snake-oil remedies, obesity rates, particularly in North America, have risen at a startling rate over the last 30 years. A recent US study suggested that 'town planning' was to blame. Perhaps we need wider streets.

1980

'Channel Tunnel opens.'
The Channel Tunnel, after several abortive attempts stymied by financial problems, eventually opened in 1994.

'World satellite-navigation system completed.'
Sat Nav is commonplace in the UK, despite sometimes insisting on some rather scenic routes.

'Large-screen, thin TVs on market.'
LCD and plasma tellies are now commonplace but many still cling to the old models, which give the little men and women who live inside them more room to move around in.

1981

'Televising of Parliament begins.'
Radio broadcasts of Parliament only began in 1978. In 1989, TV audiences were able to switch on to coverage of Parliament – and, 20 seconds later, switch off again.

1982

'Electronic touchlines installed at Wimbledon.'
The 'Hawk-Eye' system was first introduced at Wimbledon in 2007. The tantrums continued.

1984

'Simple surgery devised for contact lens implants to replace spectacles.'
The official go-ahead for laser eye surgery was given in America in 1995, allowing contact lenses to plip-plop into oblivion for many Americans.

1985

'Last British foxhound pack disbanded through lack of game and country.'
Fox-hunting was banned in the UK in 2005. This was not for lack of game and country, but for lack of love of posh Basil Brush-botherers.

1986

'First *Homo sapiens* grown to full term artificially in a laboratory.'
Artificial organs, such as a liver in 2006, have been created in laboratories, and an ear was grown on a mouse in 1989, but that's about as far as we've got.

1987

'Control of arteriosclerosis and heart disease.'
In 2006, official statistics showed that heart disease was the biggest killer in England and Wales, accounting for the

deaths of one in five men and one in six women in 2005.

1988
'US manned landing on Mars.'

Sadly, our tin helpers the robots have stymied manned missions to Mars. It is argued that, in any future expedition, they would be able to perform the same tasks as humans on the Martian surface, but at a fraction of the expense. Driving astronaut wages down, that's what they're doing . . .

'First ape taught to communicate in English.'

'Worldwide telephone dialling.'

Worldwide telephone dialling? Gosh! Long available, but apes are still, as yet, not in a position to run up bills themselves.

1989
'Surgical grafting of permanent, mechanical-limb replacements achieved.'

Mind-controlled human prosthetics were first developed in 2003.

'Socially acceptable narcotic drugs widely used.'

The narcotic drug called nicotine was officially declared socially unacceptable when cigarettes were banned in most public places in Britain in 2007.

1990
'Last national morning newspaper closes down.'

The *Sunday Correspondent*, launched in 1989, closed in 1990 following a last-ditch attempt to go tabloid. However, that year also saw the launch of the *Independent on Sunday*. So there you go.

1993
'Average national working week: 22.33 hours.'

The 1993 Working Time Directive set a Europe-wide 48-hour maximum working week and laid down requirements for rest and leave periods. And we were grateful. 22.33 hours? Parallel-universe luxury . . .

1994
'Establishment of world computer-information bank.'

Give the Burkster some credit on this one. In July 1994, *Time* magazine's cover story examined 'The Strange New World of the Internet'.

DIARY OF THE FUTURE

1995

'Domestic videophone available.'

Between 1992 and 1995, computer giant AT&T marketed the 'Videophone 2500' on sale for upwards of $1,000. Its limited availability did not compensate for its expense. Only with the rise of the mobile phone and such devices as Skype on the Internet did 'video-phoning' become at all widespread.

1996

'Legislation to abolish the use of coal and oil as fuels for heating.'

This year did indeed see much wrangling as regards the part played by fossil fuels in global warming. This was followed in 1997 by the Kyoto Procotol, which saw nations agree to reduce their greenhouse gas emissions. However, American multinationals were among those who successfully lobbied against doing anything at all to reduce emissions: it was business as usual for the US.

1999

'Creation of intelligent artificial life achieved.'

Despite fevered speculation, Artificial Intelligence is a good deal further off than is popularly imagined. As one writer put it, go to any AI research plant and, in terms of complexity and capability, you will find nothing remotely as advanced or complex as the brain of the security guard in the lobby.

2008

'Bank of England withdraws cash and notes in favour of credit card economy.'

The folding green stuff is still legal tender but the credit card has driven away the personal cheque: institutions such as London Underground and Sainsbury's no longer accept them.

2016

'2000th edition of *Tomorrow's World*.'

Tomorrow's World was cancelled in 2003. But then, for those with dominion over time itself, there is always hope. Ask *Dr Who* . . .